Not Just Talking

Helping your baby communicate – from day one

SIOBAN BOYCE

CONTENTS

= Particularly relevant to newborn babies

AUTHOR'S INTRODUCTION

The development of communication is an amazing process.
Every parent longs to hear their child talking. However,
it does not signal the start of communication.

BACKGROUND

When I trained as a Speech and Language Therapist in the 1970s we were told only once in three years that 60–90 per cent of communication is non-verbal — facial expressions, body language, reading situations and so on. These skills form the basis of every effective conversation, but we were taught no more than that because in those days non-verbal communication developed naturally as part of the daily life of babies and toddlers. Our training concentrated entirely on spoken language.

In the 1980s I became aware that children referred to me for assessment could talk well but were not communicating. They had difficulty making friends, behaving as expected, getting the best out of school and communicating about their emotions. Nobody appeared to have the answer.

Having read the available research, I saw that there had to be a connection between some of the basic things that babies do in their first few months and the development of the ability to communicate well. I also realised that changes in society might have affected the way children acquire fundamental skills.

What no one seemed to be talking about was the importance of the early development of non-verbal skills. These are essential tools because they help children know how to talk effectively, how to behave appropriately, how to recognise emotions in others and themselves, how to make and keep friends and how to benefit fully from their education.

WHY THIS BOOK IS DIFFERENT

Books for parents on the development of communication concentrate almost entirely on spoken language. But children who can talk might still have a communication problem, and difficult behaviour can be linked to their lack of non-verbal skills. This is becoming an increasingly common phenomenon.

This book focuses only on the period *before* your baby starts to talk — the time in which babies develop skills to underpin their spoken language. If they don't develop these skills, they might find it hard to get on at school or later in life. The good news is that with the aid of this book you can help your baby to become a happy and confident communicator.

WHO THIS BOOK IS AIMED AT

Not Just Talking is written for parents who are expecting or have just had a new baby. It is also relevant for those whose baby is older because it is never too late to start promoting these skills — you just have to work a bit harder at it. Midwives, health visitors and doctors will also find it useful as the first book to explain how non-verbal communication skills develop in babies.

Siobhan Boyce

A modern malady

How changes in society are affecting our children

Why is it that nowadays children are failing to develop skills in non-verbal communication – gesture, intonation, situational understanding, and so on? The simple answer is that since the 1960s the way we live our daily lives has changed and the things that help our babies develop these skills are no longer so readily available. Today's parents are given very little guidance on how to focus on these skills.

HOW DO BABIES LEARN NON-VERBAL COMMUNICATION SKILLS?

Basically, babies need to spend a great deal of time watching many different examples of people communicating face to face. They need daily experience of observing competent communicators throughout the first five years of life. In the past, nobody had to focus on developing such non-verbal communication skills as understanding and using body language and facial expression because they developed well alongside the progress of spoken communication (even boys, who find this area of communication challenging, had time to develop these skills before school). Today, it is very different.

CHANGES AFTER THE BIRTH

Many more babies than in the past now go into special care and are separated from their parents for the first few days or weeks. By the time they are out of the incubator the babies may have lost a natural drive they have to look for faces (see pages 6–7 for the significance of this), and parents will have to focus much more on encouraging this instinct. Most advice is to ensure bonding with your baby, but communication skills are far more important and should be your first concern. Bonding is only possible through communication.

THE WAY WE TALK TO OUR BABIES

In recent years 'baby talk' has had a bad press. However, as *Not Just Talking* will demonstrate, talking to babies simply and with an exaggerated intonation pattern is the only way for them to learn to recognise and understand many non-verbal methods of communicating. Once babies have learned to understand

An old-fashioned pram
This is how babies used to travel! See how the baby is almost at the same level as his mother. This means that he is easily able to see her talking to others, while having a good view of everything around him.

these big expressions, they can start to understand the subtle methods we use to express our emotions.

CHANGES IN FAMILY LIFE

In the past, non-verbal communication skills were mostly developed at the family meal table (see pages 30–31) and in the pram (see pages 20–21). These were everyday opportunities for babies and toddlers to observe different types of conversations. Children who experience only one type of conversation will grow up being able to communicate only in that one style.

A baby does not come with a manual, and, if you are on your own as parents, it can be daunting. In the past the extended family provided experience and support. Although children in single parent families may have fewer opportunities to observe two-way conversations, with only a little effort you can ensure they develop every bit as well as children brought up by two adults. And you need have no concerns about using a childminder: as long as the childminder is giving the children opportunities to watch conversations, they will not be disadvantaged.

CHANGES IN SHOPPING HABITS

Think about the way we shop. Now, we shop in anonymous supermarkets, where people rarely talk, or on the internet. This is a long way from the days when a visit to the butcher, baker or chemist was an opportunity to talk to shopkeepers and friends — with the baby in the pram observing the different conversations.

TELEVISION – A NEW PERSPECTIVE

The signals from people's non-verbal communication are too subtle for babies to pick up on a television screen and so, although they may appear to enjoy what they see, television will not help them make good sense of what is going on around them. Try not to use television to occupy babies and very young toddlers. It is much better for them to watch and hear you talking about what you are doing. Babies need to watch and learn from real people doing real things close to them.

AS YOUR CHILD GROWS

Finally, let's touch on other things that affect children as they grow. Playing every day with friends gives children the opportunity to broaden their experience of communication in its widest sense — which is useful for future situations. Nowadays, sadly, it is often thought to be unsafe for children to play outside for long periods unsupervised, but do be aware that computers and televisions in their bedrooms take them away from the family, where they can learn from watching and participating in everyday situations. Try to maintain a variety of family activities.

FOCUS POINTS

★ *Changes in society have made it hard for babies to develop vital communication skills.*

★ *It doesn't really matter who babies watch as long as the conversations are close to them.*

★ *TVs and computers do not help develop these essential communication skills.*

The first 24 hours

A fascination for faces – how it all begins

Most of us know that babies are born with natural instincts. The palmar grasp reflex, for instance, when a baby curls his fingers around your finger in a tight grip, may be inherited from our tree-dwelling ancestors. But how many new parents know that in the first few hours after birth their baby also has an amazingly strong desire to look at faces? Or that this fascination for faces is a crucial first step in the development of skills that will enable him to communicate effectively for life?

THE MOMENT OF BIRTH

Immediately a baby is born he does two things, both of which are part and parcel of becoming a good communicator for the rest of his life.

❶ He starts to scream. By doing so he starts to breathe, but he is also learning to coordinate the movement of his vocal cords. If he is to be able to speak clearly later on, he will have to develop this control, along with the movement and coordination of his tongue, lips and soft palate, before he starts to use words.

❷ When he has stopped screaming, the newborn baby starts to look around him. What he is looking for is things that are face-shaped, that is, round, with lines and dots for features. He just wants to see faces, and it is important that new parents know how vital it is to encourage this interest.

When we see our baby searching for faces, we cannot help but respond, but if for some reason the baby does not show any interest in faces, we as parents must know what to do.

WHY ARE FACES IMPORTANT?

Think what might happen if your five-year-old talked to his teacher in the way he talks to his eight-year-old sister. Think too about what might happen if he doesn't recognise when his teacher first begins to feel annoyed by his behaviour and only takes notice when she has got to the point of being absolutely furious. Life will not be easy for him.

Your child needs to be able to recognise the difference between a wide range of emotions, including happiness, sadness, boredom and anger. He also needs to understand degrees of emotion: are you a little bit sad or absolutely distraught? He must be able to tell the differences – and the similarities – in the way different people express the same feeling.

If he has learned to do all this by the time he meets his first teacher, he will recognise when she is becoming slightly annoyed and will change his behaviour so that she is happy with him.

If your child is to learn these skills by the time he is about five, he needs to look at hundreds of different faces making hundreds of different expressions. He will need to see as many adults as possible make exaggeratedly happy, sad, bored and angry expressions – exaggerated

Look at me
This picture shows how focused the baby is on her father's attentive face. Her fascination for faces means she will see all kinds of facial expressions and will then have a go at making them herself.

about 30cm (12in) away. When he looks at you, stick your tongue out at him. Repeat this expression a few times. As long as he is gazing intently at you, he should gradually start to try to stick his tongue out, imitating your expression. Your baby's vision is not developed enough at birth to make out fine detail but, even in the first day, he will be able to see the principal features of a face and he will observe this movement.

This exercise not only helps develop your baby's interest in faces, but also encourages imitation, which is another important communication skill. You can try sticking your tongue out at your baby any time during the first two or three months, but in terms of encouraging facial interest and familiarity, the earlier you are able to do this the better.

Be sure to tell other people what you are doing and why your baby might stick his tongue out at them or you could cause a few other expressions – raised eyebrows, for instance!

because babies learn to recognise these feelings better if they are loud and obvious.

In other words, your baby needs to maintain the interest in faces that he has at birth. A baby's natural instinct to search for faces fades after 24 hours unless it is stimulated. So the more you can encourage your newborn to look at faces in those first few hours after his birth, the better. Of course, this may not always be practicable – perhaps because one or both of you is very sleepy after a difficult birth or because your baby is in an incubator. Don't worry – it is never too late to encourage your baby's interest in faces, but it is only during the first 24 hours that he will actually be looking for faces.

TRY THIS!
Once things have settled down after the birth, hold your baby in front of you so that you are looking directly at his face. You need to be quite close to him,

FOCUS POINTS

★ *There is a 24-hour window after birth when your baby is actively seeking out faces.*

★ *This instinct will fade if your baby is unable to do this for any reason, for example if he is too sleepy or in an incubator.*

★ *It is hard to re-awaken this desire to look for faces, but once you realise how important it is, it can be done.*

What is my baby telling me?

The first attempt at communication

Your baby will start to communicate from the earliest days of her life. She will do this through the sounds she makes, what she looks at and, as she begins to control the movements of her body, a range of gestures. Communication begins very subtly and grows each day as the interaction between you flourishes. Let her communicate – listen to her, watch her – and you will begin to understand what she is trying to say. Without words, she needs to use a variety of sounds to tell you what she means.

DISTINGUISH HER DIFFERENT CRIES
Research has shown that babies are born with the ability to produce cries of differing pitch, volume, length and urgency. Each one means something different. Start to listen out for the differences. Does your baby cry in the same way when she is tired as she does when she is hungry or has a wet nappy? Listen to how she cries, preferably in a calm atmosphere, and you will begin to understand what she is telling you. You will soon know what she wants and will not have to try everything before you find out what she is really asking for! This will make your life, and your baby's, a lot calmer and easier.

LISTEN AND WAIT
Try not to rush to your baby whenever she starts to cry. Stop as you approach, and listen: is she quieter because she has heard you coming? Look around: is she cold because she has kicked off her blankets? Has something startled her? Is she wet and wanting a change of nappy? She needs your help to develop the ability to express different feelings. By not picking her up immediately you will

be giving her that help: she will have the chance to develop her different cries and you will learn to recognise and respond to them.

Your baby also needs to practise crying in different ways to develop her vocal skills. She will need to exercise her vocal cords a lot as she grows. By the time she starts to talk, she will need to be able to control changes in the vibration of her vocal cords. This is important because it helps her vary the tone and volume of her speech, a vital skill for effective communication. For more on this, see page 29.

NOTICE WHAT SHE LOOKS AT
It is important to notice what your baby is looking at. When she looks around and tries to focus on something, talk about what she sees and what it does. Pick it up and show it to her. 'It's a yellow car. It's like Mummy's car. It goes beep beep.'

This will also give your baby the experience of initiating a conversation. She began by looking and you then responded by showing and talking. She is encouraged to do it again.

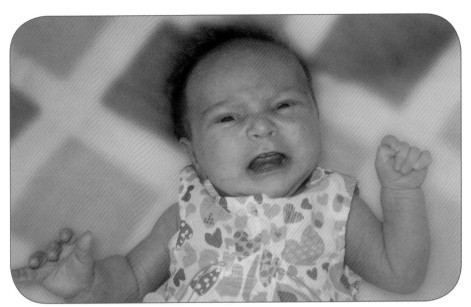

What is she trying to say to you?

She's crying. Listen, look and you will soon pick up whether she needs her nappy changed or has a pain. This baby's arms are thrashing about and her cry is loud and persistent – this might help you know how upset she is.

AS YOUR BABY STARTS TO MOVE

Once your baby can move her body, her range of experiences will quickly expand. She will have different things to communicate about. Make sure you respond to these different situations in the following way.

Each time you are able to make sense of the sound your baby is making – by picking up on other, non-verbal clues – use a word or short phrase to describe what is happening. For example, you might say 'You're hurt' if she has hit herself on something and is crying or, if she is being tickled, 'You're laughing'. Emphasise the main word in the phrase (in this case, 'hurt' or 'laughing') by stressing it and saying it a bit louder than the other words. She will hear the emphasised word and link it to what is happening at the time you say it. You need to be consistent in the words you use, so that she hears the same one over and over again linked to the same or similar experiences. This will also apply when your baby is learning to talk (see pages 39 and 41).

FOCUS POINTS

★ *Stop and listen to your baby crying before you pick her up.*

★ *Say what you think she is crying about – use the same words for each situation.*

★ *Watch what she is looking at and talk to her about it.*

Structure and routine

Help your baby make sense of his daily routine

Birth, for your baby, means entering a world of chaos. He will need to be able to make sense of what is happening around him if he is to communicate effectively. To do this, he will have to develop certain skills, such as recognising when things start and finish, and he will learn these more easily when there is a clear structure and routine in his life, leading to calm and predictability.

MAKING SENSE OF HIS DAY

First, you need to help your baby understand what is going to be happening to him. You do not need to be rigid in your organisation, but providing some sort of structure and routine to the day will help your baby in many ways: it will help him to feel more secure, develop confidence and learn to predict, all of which are important for effective communication.

Make sure your baby knows exactly what is happening next and when that activity is finished. He will need to learn how to move onto another activity and to recognise from what you are doing what is going to happen in different situations, for example nappy changing, feeding, bathing. Structure is a clear way of showing the order of the day. So, for example, he learns that it is time to go to sleep when he is put in his cot, kissed goodnight and the light goes off.

Break your baby's day into sleeping, eating, nappy changing, bathing and other activities. The latter can be anything from going out for a walk, lying on his back gazing at the ceiling or listening to a musical toy. One activity can be followed by another, fitted round his basic needs of sleeping,

eating and nappy changing. Don't forget that he will want to play too!

WHAT IS HE TRYING TO TELL YOU?

Your baby might be crying because he is hungry, because he wants his nappy changed or because he needs to sleep, but there may be other reasons why he his crying. For example, babies have a limited attention span and can easily be over-stimulated, which might make them cry. Your baby might simply be trying to tell you he wants to do something different. It doesn't necessarily mean he wants to move from activity to sleeping or eating. He might just want to do something more or less stimulating, or just plain different.

TIME FOR YOU

It is really important to give yourself breaks, if only to sleep. So while your baby is asleep, have some time for yourself. There might be a hundred things to do that can't be done while he is awake, but at one point in the day, at least, make time to do something just for you — relax!

When he shows signs of being restless or starts to cry, stop the activity and try something else. Maybe take him out for a walk or play a lap game with him. Or does he want to sleep?

START AND FINISH

Not knowing when something is beginning or ending makes your baby feel anxious. Being able to recognise starts and finishes helps him to stay calm. It is also one of the first steps towards prediction (see pages 16–17). When you have a clear structure to the day, there are plenty of opportunities for you to help your baby learn that things have a beginning and an end. Think of each activity your baby does as having a start and a finish.

Whenever you do something with your baby, for example changing his nappy, feeding him or taking him out for a walk, make sure that you signal the beginning and end of the activity very clearly. The signal could be a sound, something your baby can see, or a word or phrase. As he grows, this will help him notice

Bath time
This baby is looking directly at her mother. This is a perfect time to talk about what is happening and what will happen next. You could make up a bathtime song!

for himself the subtle clues that tell us that something has started and finished. Sometimes one activity can be broken into two or three elements – signal the start and finish of each of these different parts of the activity.

Get into the habit of saying 'It's time for …', and at the end say '… is finished'. You can also sign the name of the activity (see pages 32–33). Let us say the activity is bath time. Keep to the same routine each day. Show him an item at the start, for example the bath, and say 'It's bath time'. When it's time to get him out of the bath say (and sign) 'Bath is finished'. The signal for bath time being over could be the water

Here it comes
Hold the spoon in front of your baby's mouth, wait for her to open her mouth and say 'Here it comes!' Look at how this baby is focused on the spoon – she wants to eat.

going down the plughole – make the noise of the water disappearing.

You can then move on to drying and dressing. Signal the end of each routine with an action or object that will help

CRANIAL OSTEOPATHY

If there has been a difficult or stressful birth and your baby is unsettled, is screaming or has colic, once you have checked with your doctor, it is worth seeing a cranial osteopath for an assessment. Cranial osteopathy is a very gentle treatment that can help reduce stresses and strains and is especially useful with very young babies. Contact the College of Osteopaths to find a registered osteopath near you.

You can use phrases and rhymes to draw attention to the beginnings and ends of activities. When your baby is finishing his food: say 'All gone' with an exaggerated tone, raising your arms above your head.

When your baby is a bit older and you are doing a clearing-up activity, introduce a 'tidy-up' song, like this one sung to the tune of 'Jingle Bells':

Tidy-up song
Tidy-up, tidy-up, put the toys away.
Tidy-up, tidy-up, we're finished for today.
Oh, tidy-up, tidy-up, put the toys away.
For we'll get them out again
The next time that we play.

Sing this whenever you are 'tidying' anything up, from the table to his bedroom. You'll find it a very helpful routine when he gets a bit older!

Make up rhymes for other activities. Remember that rhymes and songs have non-verbal clues that help your baby understand what to do (see pages 26–27).

your baby know it is finished. Stick to the same routine and your baby will learn fast. Try not to confuse him by having items not associated with the activity in the vicinity, for example toys all over the table when it is laid for a meal. When your baby is used to the routine and shows he knows what might be happening next, you can introduce the idea of change (see pages 34–35).

STILL UNSETTLED ?
If your baby is erratic in his habits, waking at night or feeding at irregular times, helping him to make better sense of the world through the structures recommended here should result in a better routine. If not, you might just need to be more consistent and keep the signals going a bit longer. See also box (left) on cranial osteopathy.

FOCUS POINTS

★ *Structure will help your baby make sense of a complex world.*

★ *Through structure, your baby learns to predict what is about to happen and will feel secure. This will help him become an effective communicator later in life.*

★ *Signal in an obvious way the start and finish of anything your baby does.*

★ *Use rhymes and repeated phrases so your baby knows what is going to happen next.*

Give and take

The two-way process of conversations

Believe it or not, your baby will start learning how to hold conversations in the first few days and months of her life! She will do this through interaction – the two-way flow of looks, gestures, sounds and words between father and baby, sister and baby, and so on. This interaction begins when your baby has her first feed. During the first year of life she needs to enjoy interacting with others so that she develops the ability to communicate effectively.

THE ART OF CONVERSATION

Before your baby is able to talk she needs to learn about the give and take of conversations – how to wait her turn, how to respond to others, how to start a conversation. These skills are very subtle, but they are the foundation of effective communication. They are difficult to acquire later in life, so the time you spend helping your baby now will be very well spent.

THE EARLY DAYS OF INTERACTING

As we have seen on pages 6–7, babies are keen to look for faces. This is an important part of learning how to interact. Making faces and noises that interest your baby will encourage her to look at your face.

A good time to do this is when she is feeding. At the start of a feed your baby will suck without pausing but, once she has taken the edge off her hunger, she will pause now and then. The pauses will become more frequent and longer as the feed progresses. Your baby will look at you, and you will look at her in return. Once your baby knows that you will return her gaze, she will look for more interaction with you. She will start to enjoy sending a signal (the look she gives you) and receiving a reply (your look at her). Treasure these special times – you are helping to develop her conversational skills.

Always make sure you get close to your baby, so that she can see your face clearly: bend over the cot, get down on the floor with her, lift her onto your knee. When your baby is a bit older and is in a buggy or a bouncy chair, she may be low down or on the floor. You will need to get down to her level or step back so that she can see you better.

TAKING IT FURTHER

Once you are confident that she is interested in looking at you during the feed, start to make noises for her – perhaps cooing or humming sounds. Wait for her to reply. If she makes a noise at you, respond by making the same, or perhaps a different, noise.

It is important for your baby to know that what she 'says' is interesting to you. This imitation of the noises she makes is called 'mirroring' and will let your baby know that you value her attempts at communication – even if you do not always understand what they mean.

Encourage her to imitate you!
This baby is roaring at her mother, who has just made a lion noise. You can see she's loving it. Her mother pretended to be scared. This is the give and take on which conversations are based.

These exchanges should be playful. Sometimes you will lead, sometimes your baby will lead. This will encourage her to initiate communication as well as respond to you. You want her to be an independent communicator, so you need to stimulate both sides of the communication process. This will also encourage her to listen carefully — a vital skill for effective communication and learning.

The skills your baby uses to interact will continue to develop as she grows older, giving her the ability to take turns appropriately in conversations. She will gradually come to understand — and take pleasure in — the give and take of successful conversations. It will also help her to know when it is her turn to talk if she also understands body language and vocal clues such as stress and intonation.

FOCUS POINTS

★ *Make contact with your baby during feeding — respond to her when she looks at you.*

★ *Enjoy interacting with your baby.*

★ *Respond to her attempts to communicate by imitating the sounds she makes.*

★ *This skill is the foundation for turn-taking in conversation.*

Prediction

Learning that one thing leads to another

We all know how anxious we feel when we can't predict what's going to happen – after an interview, for example, when we don't know whether we've got the job or not. Children who can't predict feel like this most of the time. And when we are anxious, communication is often the first thing to let us down: we become tongue-tied and struggle to express ourselves. To communicate successfully, your child must be able to predict what is going to happen next.

THE LEARNING CURVE

Your baby is not born with an ability to know what is going to happen next. He has to develop this very complex skill over the first few years of life.

Being able to predict will help your baby become a good communicator because:

❶ Instead of feeling anxious about what might happen next, he will feel confident and therefore better able to communicate.

❷ He will know how people might react to what he is about to say and will know what to say so that they don't get upset or cross.

TEACHING YOUR BABY TO PREDICT

The ability to predict will develop only if your baby has learned that one thing might lead to another. So what can we do to help our children know what is going to happen next?

Always talk about what you are going to do with your baby, keeping the language short and simple. For example, 'We're going to put your shoes on'. Repeat simple phrases at each stage of the activity, such as 'Here it comes, here it comes'. It is very important to use a sing-song intonation, building up to the anticipated conclusion. You should also use this method when feeding solids, and at bathtime and bedtime. You will recognise the signs that he can anticipate because he will stop crying, move his body in an excited way or shriek – all signs of expectation.

FOCUS POINTS

★ *Babies have to learn that one thing follows another.*

★ *Being able to predict what's going to happen reduces anxiety and helps us communicate well.*

★ *Talk to your baby about what you are going to do, using 'here it comes' phrases.*

★ *Nursery rhymes help to develop your child's sense of expectation.*

★ *Babies learn to predict from intonation patterns used in games such as 'Peekaboo'.*

AN EXERCISE TO ENHANCE PREDICTION SKILLS

Make fun out of situations that have different stages to them – nappy changing is ideal. It takes place several times every day and offers many opportunities to play 'Here it comes!' games. You should exaggerate your intonation as you talk your baby through each stage. She will soon learn to predict what's about to happen.

Starting the activity

As you pick up your baby, tell her it's time to change her nappy. Throughout the process, it's very important to use a rhythmical intonation, stressing each stage and emphasising its final conclusion.

Taking off her trousers

Take her trousers off slowly. At each stage – unbuttoning, pulling them down – repeat 'Off come the trousers!' When they are fully off, say 'Trousers off!' and hold them up so your baby can see them.

Cleaning her bottom

As you start to clean her bottom, hold the wipe up so she can see it and say 'Here comes the wipe!'. Repeat this in two or three stages as the wipe gets closer and closer. Finally say 'Now I'm cleaning your bottom!'

Putting on the new nappy

Make sure your baby knows what you are about to do by letting her see the nappy moving towards her as you tell her it's coming. As you put her clothes back on say, 'On go the trousers!'

Making sense of it all
Developing non-verbal understanding

Once your baby is doing more than sleeping and eating, she will become increasingly aware of what is happening around her. She needs to develop her non-verbal understanding through her everyday activities. Progress is relentless. You need a good idea of what to do.

FACIAL EXPRESSIONS AGAIN!

On pages 6–7 we discussed your baby's first step towards learning what faces tell you. We also saw how in her early years she needs not only to recognise the difference between facial expressions such as surprised and puzzled, but also to understand the different levels of emotion, for example elated and content. Remember, she will have a much better chance of picking up these subtle nuances if you exaggerate your expressions. Keeping your expressions clear, even now that she is a bit older, will not hamper her communication development or be 'babying' her and, if you stop doing this, she might not pick up on vital clues to help develop her skills.

There are some excellent board books by Margaret Miller and Roberta Grobel Intrater (see page 42) that will help your baby recognise facial expressions in other babies. Choose books with pictures of real people showing different emotions. Drawings or pictures of animals are not so good. If you can't get hold of books with photographs of people, you could take your own pictures.

Nursery rhymes (see pages 26–27) are also very helpful because most can be said or sung close to your baby's face, perhaps with her sitting on your lap. Another excellent feature is that they include exaggerated and sometimes unexpected facial expressions, as well as gestures to help baby make sense of what the face is saying. Nursery rhymes provide exactly the experience your baby needs. Don't be shy of singing them many times a day – the more the better.

MODELLING BEHAVIOUR

Your baby learns to understand and do things herself because she watches you so intently. What you are doing is

Fascinating faces
Just look how engrossed this baby is in her book of pictures of babies making different faces.

'modelling' behaviour to her. If she sees you do something, she is more likely to try it herself. This is called 'imitation'. Remember that your baby will imitate *any* behaviour, including behaviour that will *not* help develop her communication skills, such as not looking at people when talking to them. So show her behaviour that you *do* want her to copy.

By now you will have made sure that she is looking at you a lot. You need to encourage her to continue looking at people when they are talking. Whenever you speak to her, try to put your face at the same level as hers. If she sees you do this many times a day she will learn that she must look at people when communicating. She will be building up her store of knowledge about the differences and similarities in facial expressions. It's important this is well developed by the time she starts school. Remember, if you talk to her and don't look at her, you are modelling behaviour that will restrict her ability to know what different types of facial expression and body language mean.

KEEP LANGUAGE SIMPLE AND CLEAR
Here are some tips to help your baby understand what you say to her.
❶ Make sure the atmosphere is calm and relatively quiet when you talk to her. If there is a lot of background sound, such as the television or her siblings playing noisily, she won't be able to focus on what you are saying.
❷ Keep what you say short and simple: 'Daddy's shoes' rather than 'Look over there, Daddy has left his shoes by the chair'. Again, this simple talk is not 'baby language'; it is the language she needs if she is to make sense of the barrage of speech sounds coming at her.

UNDERSTANDING SITUATIONS
Now your baby needs to recognise the clues that tell her what situation she is in, for example the bathroom or the garden. Talk to her about what you see in these everyday situations. Draw her attention to the things that identify places and situations: 'Here we are in the bathroom. Look at the basin. Look at the bath.' Point to each one and sign (see pages 32–33) as you say the name.

When you see a different bathroom in someone else's house, talk about the similarities and the differences: 'Their bath is blue' or 'Look at the round basin'. She needs to understand the idea of 'bathroom' from common clues. She will then be able to recognise the same situation in different circumstances.

Don't forget how important structure is in helping your baby understand what is happening now and what will happen next (see pages 10–13). Clear visual signposts will help develop her understanding of the world.

FOCUS POINTS

★ *Make sure your baby looks at your face whenever you are talking.*

★ *Show her photos of people making different expressions; talk about them and make the sounds that go with them.*

★ *Model the behaviour you want your baby to use.*

★ *Make sure she can recognise situations from the visual clues.*

Baby equipment

How it can help or hinder learning to communicate

Since the 1960s there have been enormous changes in the equipment used to transport babies and toddlers. These were made with the best intentions, to make life easier for parents or because it was thought that babies would develop interest in the world by facing forward in a pushchair. The fact is that, if they are to develop the skills they need to make sense of the world and to communicate with others, babies need to spend as much time as possible watching adults in conversation.

MAKE SURE YOUR BABY CAN SEE YOU TALKING

Whenever you are holding a conversation with someone, try to ensure your baby is present and can see both of you speaking and listening to one another. Before he is able to sit on his own, the only way of doing this is to carry him or hold him on your knee, but when he can sit by himself try to have him high enough to see you easily — a high chair is ideal or, when you are out and about, a pushchair with a seat that faces you.

THE BUGGY (AND ANY EQUIPMENT THAT KEEPS BABY AT KNEE HEIGHT)

Before the buggy was invented, a baby — often until he was four or five years old — was likely to be in a pram, facing his parents (see picture on page 4). The introduction of the buggy made life easier for parents, but in a buggy the baby faced forward and, because he now had his back to his parents, he was not able to observe them engaged in everyday conversations. Of course, no one told parents how important this was to the development of non-verbal communication skills. So they were not able to make an informed choice; nor

were they given advice on how to compensate for this key change.

It is probably the buggy more than anything else that has reduced the amount of time babies spend watching people hold conversations. Sitting in a pram, a baby can see his mother and, most likely, whoever she might be talking to. In a forward-facing buggy, the baby will at best see only one side of the conversation.

We have all seen parents pushing their baby in the buggy chatting away to their child while unable to see his face. Talking to a baby when you cannot see his face suggests to him that you don't need to look at people when you are talking to them. Babies learn most of their communication skills — both verbal and non-verbal — through watching people who are demonstrating good conversational skills. (See pages 18–19 for more on the benefits of 'modelling'.)

As we have seen, to become a good speaker and listener, your baby must learn that he has to look at the person he is talking to. If he doesn't, he will not be able to pick up the non-verbal clues in their conversation — a frown, a smile, a nod of the head, a wave of the hand.

Facing her mummy
Look at how intently this baby is looking at the conversation between her mummy and a friend. She is only able to do this because her buggy faces the person pushing it.

You need to show him how to do this by looking at him whenever you talk to him and letting him see your face when you talk to other people. Remember that talking on your mobile might confuse your baby as he won't know who you are talking to – he could be forgiven for thinking you are talking to him!

To overcome the disadvantage of the forward-facing buggy, you need make only small changes in your behaviour. Whenever you hold a conversation with anyone while your baby is in the buggy, turn the buggy round and make sure that you are facing the person and that your baby can see you both. Even when you are talking on the phone make sure he can see you.

If you are buying a buggy, bear in mind that a high seat makes it easier for your baby to see your face and the faces of other people talking to you.

CAR SEATS
Another thing that limits the number of conversations your baby can watch is the fact that nowadays we depend heavily on our cars and don't walk as much as previous generations of parents. The car seat has been developed with the focus on safety. Rear-facing car seats in the front are a good choice for a new baby because he is able to look at your face while you are driving, but it won't be long before he has grown too big for a rear-facing seat. Also, these cannot be used in a car that has airbags.

The use of the car reduces the number of occasions your baby will have to watch two or more people holding a conversation. Walking or taking the bus is not only better for the environment but gives you more opportunities for conversation, which baby can watch.

FOCUS POINTS

★ *Look at your baby when you talk to him. If necessary, turn the buggy so he can see you.*

★ *Prams are better than forward-facing buggies because your baby can watch you talk to people.*

★ *Baby needs to see your facial expressions – frowns and smiles and so on.*

★ *Adjust your body position if your baby is low down, so that he can see you well.*

Building self-awareness
Why it is relevant to communication

Your baby is not born knowing she is a unique being. She has to learn this in her first year of life. It happens gradually, and she will demonstrate this increased self-awareness by what she does and eventually by what she says. Without this skill, she will assume that everyone is thinking the same as she is and she will therefore not recognise the need for communication.

KNOWING YOU, KNOWING ME

A baby's impulse to communicate begins with the understanding that she is a separate person. As she develops, the realisation that what she has in her mind is different from what is in the minds of other people around her will help her to know what she needs to say to them.

When a baby is born she does not know she is a separate person from her parents. During the first few months of her life she will start to recognise the different people close to her and then to see that she is a distinct person too. She needs to communicate her thoughts in order to be understood. Unless this awareness that she is a separate person develops, she will not recognise that her thoughts are not shared by everyone else and that to be understood she has to communicate.

RECOGNISING HERSELF AND OTHERS

Your baby is unlikely to recognise herself in a mirror during the first six months of life. She will see her reflection and might respond to it as an interesting person, but there will be no sense of recognition.

You will also notice at around six or seven months that your baby will cry and even scream at the prospect of being handed to an unfamiliar person. You may be worried that something is wrong or that she is going backwards in her skill development. Don't be. It is an important sign that she is developing new skills and indicates that she has started to recognise the real differences between people she knows well and strangers. In time she will cling to you less as she develops her understanding of who she is and who her family and friends are.

INTRODUCE MIRRORS AND PHOTOS

Babies only learn by looking at things and making connections between what they see and what they think and feel. Your baby could go through her whole life without seeing herself if not for the presence of mirrors and photos. Both these things help her to start to recognise herself and develop a picture of herself as a person in her mind's eye. She begins to appreciate the distinction between herself and other people.

Very early on in your baby's life, start to play with mirrors — making sure that you use a safe, non-breakable

Look at me!

This baby pointed at herself in the mirror, then turned to her mother and pointed at the hair clip on her head. She then turned back to the mirror and pointed at herself. This shows she had begun to understand that the baby in the mirror was her.

mirror sold by baby equipment shops and outlets such as the Early Learning Centre. Sit in front of a mirror so you can both see each other. Make faces at her, wave at her and draw attention to yourself. Make loud noises such as 'coo-eee' or 'oo-hoo' to draw her attention to you. If you are out and about, whenever you pass a mirror or see your reflections in a window, wave at her and call her name.

The first person that your baby will learn to recognise in a mirror is you! You can notice whether or not she recognises herself (this is usually beginning to develop around six to eight months) because she will smile when she sees you but may not pay any attention to her own image in the mirror. Only when your baby starts to look at herself, smiling and babbling – that is, trying to talk to herself – or making faces at herself, will you know that she is on the way to recognising herself.

HOW TO EXTEND MIRROR PLAY

Talk to your baby about who she can see in the mirror – her brother, sister or an aunt. Talk about what you see others doing in the mirror. Play peekaboo games hiding your baby behind a cloth and pulling it off suddenly or hiding your face from her with your hands.

When your baby starts to try out different facial expressions or hand movements and looks at the mirror to check that the baby in the mirror is doing it too, then there is no doubt that she knows it's herself she sees.

Talk to your baby through the mirror: ask her what she wants for tea, or if she would like to change activity, maybe look at a book or build with bricks.

YOU AND ME

When you are talking to your baby, make special reference to anything to do with the idea of 'you' and 'me'.

Draw attention to what you are doing or going to do and what you might be feeling or thinking. Talk about the same things in relation to your baby. Tell her what she is doing or what you think she might be feeling or thinking. Talk about the same points in relationship to others in the family, for example 'Daddy is putting a jumper on — he must be cold. Are you cold, Daddy?' All of this will help her to see the differences in

SOMETHING ELSE TO TRY

You might like to develop a photo album or scrapbook that is a record of your baby's life. With lots of photos of her full face and full body doing different things, she will soon learn to recognise herself. Also, compare photos of other people, tell her the names of the people in the photos, and talk about what they are doing. Use photos of people she is familiar with and repeat the same words each time, for example 'Daddy is swimming', 'Sarah is running'. Write these words under the pictures so that other people can use the same words.

It is difficult to find books with simple pictures of people doing things, but you could make your own. For instance, you could make a separate album of granny and grandad working in the garden, doing the shopping, driving the car, eating lunch and so on.

Talking about what others are doing and comparing that with what you and your baby do, helps to develop your baby's awareness of herself as an individual.

people and will continue to develop her ideas about herself.

MOVING AWAY FROM YOU

After she has learned to crawl or walk, your baby will start to move away from you in different situations, as long as there is no one else around. This is to test out how far she can go and still know that you will be there for her. This act of distancing herself from you is another demonstration that she knows she is a separate entity from you. She will keep looking back at you to check you are still there.

MAKING YOU LAUGH

Realising that she can make people laugh is another sign that your baby understands she is a different person. Repeating behaviour that gets a response she likes is a clear sign that she is acquiring a sense of herself. Notice how she does something and laughs, then looks at you to see if you are laughing. This is a clear indication that she knows you are thinking something different: she realises that you perhaps haven't laughed at the same time. Help her develop this awareness by encouraging her to laugh about funny things that you do.

I can make you laugh!
This baby is doing things with the cup knowing that her audience is finding it funny. She continued to do this for some time, developing ideas of what she could do with it to amuse everyone.

FOCUS POINTS

★ *Your baby needs to learn who she is by first recognising her mum and dad.*

★ *Emphasise 'you' and 'me'.*

★ *Be happy when she becomes clingy, not wanting to be picked up by 'strangers' – it is a sign that this skill is developing well.*

★ *Use mirrors and photos to teach your baby to recognise herself and others.*

★ *Watch her learn how to move away from you with confidence, knowing she can always come back.*

Nursery rhymes
All the right ingredients!

Nursery rhymes have all the components necessary for developing many of the non-verbal skills. Simply by singing or reciting nursery rhymes and playing lap games with your baby as often as you can, you will be doing a huge amount to help him develop his communication skills.

WHAT MAKES NURSERY RHYMES SO IMPORTANT?
Nursery rhymes have been passed down from generation to generation and have always been hugely popular with parents as well as their children. In the old days, of course, television filled less of our day than it does now (and

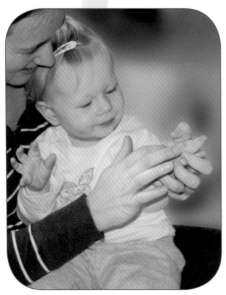

Round and round the garden
Look how focused this baby is on her hand and her mummy's hand. After saying 'One step', pause and see whether your baby giggles in anticipation of the tickle under the arm. Say the words slowly and pause after 'two steps'. Encourage her delight.

there was only one programme a day for toddlers), and much of the time that parents and their young children spent together was taken up with nursery rhymes and lap games.

Now research is proving how important nursery rhymes are, not only for the communication skills dealt with in this book but also in helping to develop pre-reading skills!

Babies and parents enjoy nursery rhymes and lap games — they are fun, help you bond with your baby and will develop his confidence. As you will see below, rhymes contain many important elements of non-verbal communication, and regular use of nursery rhymes and lap games with your baby can make a real difference to his ability to communicate effectively.

LOOK AT ME! WHAT AM I DOING?
You must make sure your face is close to your baby, so sit him on your lap or in his high chair. From this position he can see not only what your face does but also what your body is doing. Start with just one or two nursery rhymes — 'Twinkle, twinkle, little star' or 'Incey Wincey Spider'. Find one he really enjoys and repeat it often. Make sure you do all the actions. Some books of nursery rhymes show these (see page 42).

ENCOURAGING EXPECTATION AND PREDICTION

Because nursery rhymes are repetitive and engaging, your baby should soon pick up the idea of the different movements and what you are about to do. He will also learn to recognise your rising intonation pattern when reciting such rhymes as 'Round and Round the Garden' and will learn what to expect.

DEVELOPING INTONATION PATTERNS, STRESS AND RHYTHM

Intonation patterns, stress and rhythm are the non-verbal clues that we add to words to help people make better sense of what we are saying. They are the sound clues that make it possible for you to listen to the radio or talk on the telephone — situations when you cannot see the person talking.

Nursery rhymes help because all the intonation, stress and rhythm patterns are exaggerated, emphasised and repeated, so eventually your baby will pick them up. Try 'This little piggy went to market', varying intonation as much as you can and stressing 'market', 'home' and so on: 'This little piggy went to *market*, this little piggy stayed at *home*.'

LISTENER AND SPEAKER ROLES

Nursery rhymes and lap games give a baby the chance to practise, again and again, looking at people, sitting still to hear what is being said, and listening carefully. They also provide many opportunities to ask for more.

FOCUS POINTS

★ *If your baby doesn't seem to respond, don't give up. Just keep trying different rhymes until you find one that he really responds to.*

★ *Lap games where there is movement and the opportunity to choose are excellent.*

★ *Exaggerate your intonation to make it interesting and noticeable.*

Early use of non-verbal skills

Exploring touch, gesture, voice and facial expression

Alongside the development of other non-verbal skills, keep in mind that your baby will need to use her face and body to communicate to others effectively. This section will help you encourage your baby to respond to and use touch, facial expressions, vocalisations and gestures. All these simple things will also help your baby become a better listener as she grows up.

TOUCHY FEELY

In this book touching means any touch that happens between two people. It often means touching hands, or arms, but also sitting on laps. Nursery rhymes and lap games (see pages 26–27) play a huge role in your baby's learning how and when to touch.

Touching is a natural part of caring for your baby, for example while bathing her, changing her nappy and rubbing in creams to prevent nappy rash, or massaging her with oil. Through these everyday activities your baby will learn the meaning and pleasure of touch, and this will help her immensely later in life. Your baby needs to learn what touch means and how to touch others. This is a learning process that will continue right through to adolescence, when it becomes really important to know how to touch people in an appropriate way.

ENCOURAGE THE USE OF GESTURES

Gestures are general movements of the body that have meaning. To encourage

---

A LAP GAME TO ENCOURAGE TOUCH AND GESTURES

Any child I have ever played this game with has really loved it (but it is not recommended for children over about four or five if you wish to preserve your back!). Before your baby can talk, get her to point up, down or round.

Hey, little fishy in the sea

1. Pick your child up and get her to put her legs around your waist.
2. Tip her head down towards the floor and ask

'Hey, little fishy in the sea, what do you want for your tea? Up, down or round?'

3. If she chooses 'up', you throw her up in the air. For 'down', tumble her head over heels to the ground. For 'round', swirl her round like an aeroplane.
4. Finally, she gets the opportunity to ask 'more'!

your baby to use gestures you need to make yours large and noticeable! For example, when you are saying hello and and goodbye, make sure that you wave your hand clearly; when your baby finishes her food, hold your hands up in the air above your head and say with a large intonation pattern 'All gone!'; point to yourself and say 'Me', then point to your baby and say 'You'.

HOW DO BABIES' VOICES DEVELOP?

Your baby is born not knowing how to use her voice. During the period from birth until she learns to talk, she will have to exercise her vocal cords and all the muscles needed for speech if she is to ensure that she can start talking at some point between about 12 and 36 months of age. The crying, gurgling, laughing and cooing sounds that she makes from a very early age help her to gain fine control of her vocal cords.

As we saw on pages 8–9, if you don't rush to pick your baby up the moment she starts crying, you give her the chance to learn to vary her cry by using different pitch, intonation, volume and urgency. The ability to change pitch, intonation and volume helps her express different meanings, and she will develop one cry for when she is hungry, one for when for she is in pain, one for when she is bored, and so on. Babies who are not given this opportunity early on to develop different cries might find it hard to vary their voice for speech later on.

When your baby coos and gurgles, you can help her voice development first by copying any sounds she makes and then by encouraging her to try new sounds — perhaps by changing the rhythm of your coo back to her or by varying the length of the coo.

HELP YOUR BABY BABBLE

Babbling refers to the noises that your baby starts to make from the age of about six months. They are very different from the early gurgles and coos. They sound much more like speech, because the babble will have the intonation pattern of your baby's mother tongue. Babbling will help your baby to develop this intonation, so that by the time she is talking she will be very good at it. For more on cooing and babbling, see pages 38–39.

ENCOURAGE FACIAL EXPRESSIONS

Make sure your baby can make facial expressions for herself. She needs to exercise her facial muscles to help her gain control for the very fine movements necessary, and this can be done by making large, exaggerated expressions. Make sure you also expand the range of expressions that she sees — thoughtful, worried, proud, excited and so on — and encourage her to imitate these. Remember, you need to exaggerate the expression to make it noticeable for your baby. And don't forget those nursery rhymes and lap games!

FOCUS POINTS

★ *Make sure you are touching your baby and encourage her to feel your arms and face.*

★ *Listen to your baby's cry from a very early stage. It will tell you a lot.*

★ *Exaggerate gestures such as waving goodbye and pointing.*

Eating together
Why family mealtimes are so important

As your baby gets older, he will start to eat solids, and this will change the way the two of you interact while he feeds. He will soon be able to sit in a high chair at the table, rather than on your lap, which will significantly increase the number of opportunities he has to observe conversations taking place. The process of eating is one of the richest areas of your baby's life for developing non-verbal conversational skills. This section will help you to look at the family mealtime in a completely different way, showing you how beneficial these everyday conversations are.

HOW CAN SPOON-FEEDING HELP CONVERSATION DEVELOP?

The transition to spoon-feeding should be another step towards your baby's enjoyment of food and eating. It will also bring plenty of opportunities for you to help him develop his interacting skills. As he finishes each spoonful, he will look at you and use gesture and facial expression to let you know that he is enjoying his food and wants some more. Alternatively, he might just spit it out — which, of course, is his way of telling you that he does not want any more.

As discussed on pages 16–17, prediction is an important skill, and one that you should promote in your baby. There is a great deal of prediction involved in the use of a spoon to feed your baby. Start by talking to your baby about filling the spoon — for example, say 'Look, yoghurt on the spoon'. As you move the spoon towards his mouth, say 'Here it comes ... here it comes ... and open wide'. Then add whatever you like as the spoon goes into his mouth — perhaps 'Yum, yum'.

HOW DOES THE FAMILY MEAL TABLE HELP?

When your baby sits at the family meal table with lively conversation going on around him, he will see the smiles, frowns and looks of surprise that indicate people's feelings. He will notice people leaning forward to show interest in what someone is saying, using their hands to emphasise a point or lowering their voice to share a secret — all the varieties of intonation and style that convey meaning and intention.

The way your baby learns is through watching adults and older brothers and sisters (see pages 18–19). This gives him an understanding of how to behave in different situations.

One of the most important things to model to your baby is that while communicating he must look at people. Think about this: when your family is sitting at the table and the older members are watching the television, conversation takes second place. What you are demonstrating to your baby or toddler in his high chair is that you can eat, talk and watch the television at the same time — without needing to look at the person you are talking to. So, please turn the television off while eating at the table. Let the conversation flow!

SIGNAL THE BEGINNINGS AND ENDINGS OF ACTIVITIES

Making the beginning and end of activities very obvious helps your baby learn to spot the more subtle clues that will, as he grows into a toddler, help him to predict what might happen next. In its turn, this will make him confident and happy. (See pages 10–13.)

Think about the process of laying a table. The act of laying the table tells us that a meal is on the way. We understand, when we see that the table has been laid, that the meal will be served up shortly. Sitting your baby at the table in a high chair before you start laying the table, allows him to see the gradual build-up to setting the places on the table before the food arrives. He learns to notice that the meal has not yet started but will be able to predict that it is about to happen. He may also hear his mother or father

confirm this by calling out 'Come and sit down. Lunch is ready.'

The arrival of plates full of food signals the start of the first course. Then, as the food disappears, the baby learns that things are getting close to a finish. Maybe the parents might say to the children 'Finish your food', reinforcing through words and intonation pattern what is going on. At the end of the first course, the empty plates are taken away and, because he sees that there is still a spoon at each person's place, the baby learns that there is more food coming. Soon he will learn to predict that it is pudding that's arriving next!

HELP YOUR BABY TO DEVELOP MANY DIFFERENT TYPES OF CONVERSATIONAL STYLE

Because your baby is sitting watching many conversations, he is going to see people communicating in many ways: they may be happy, sad, enthusiastic, secretive or angry, for example. From this he will learn that he needs to talk to people in different ways, depending on the person, the situation and what they are talking about. Babies who observe only one style of communication tend to communicate in a limited fashion themselves.

Eating round a table
This baby can see her father and brother eating their food. This is a good model for how she will need to sit and eat at the table when she is older. Also, she can see all the signs of starting and finishing a meal for three people – not just her own.

Sign to your baby

Baby learns to understand signs

Signing – using signs made with your hands to represent words – can help you and your baby communicate successfully in the years before she is able to understand and use words fluently. The first step is to teach your baby what the signs mean. This is easier than it sounds.

HOW DOES SIGNING HELP MY BABY UNDERSTAND WHAT I AM SAYING?

Until your baby is able to understand words, the only clues she has to what you are saying to her are your facial expression, tone of voice and gestures. But these are sophisticated clues, and because early on she does not yet have the skill or experience to interpret them fully, she is not always able to make good sense of what is going on around her. Signing will help to bridge the gap until she is able to do so.

If, for example, your baby doesn't know that you are putting her in the car to drive home for tea but thinks you are setting off to do some more shopping, she may well get upset or have a tantrum. Unable to use speech, she communicates her frustration and confusion in the only way she can – by getting upset and angry. If, instead of not knowing what is happening next, your baby understands that you are going to drive home for tea, she will (if that is what she wants to do!) stay calm and contented. Babies can learn to understand signs such as 'home' and 'tea' at a surprisingly young age.

TEACHING YOUR BABY

Start as early as possible (within the first month), making signs and saying the word associated with the sign. You do not need to use signs from programmes such as British Deaf Signs or Makaton. You can invent your own – your baby will stop using them as soon as she can talk. As long as you use the same sign each time you use a particular word, for example 'daddy' when daddy is there or you are talking about daddy, your baby will learn that this sign means daddy.

Start with words that are meaningful to your baby. Make a list of words that she might need during a typical day. These must relate to real objects or people. For example, 'mummy', 'daddy', 'car', 'dinner', 'book'. There is no point in teaching your baby signs that she will hardly ever need to understand,

FOCUS POINTS

★ *Signing helps bridge the gap between non-verbal and verbal means of communication.*

★ *Teach your baby only words that she will use on a regular basis.*

★ *Look at your baby's face, make the sign, say the word.*

like 'pencil' or 'ladder'. Words such as 'drink', 'food', 'nappy' and 'sleep' will be useful for most babies.

The next stage is to introduce more complex signs, such as 'more', 'next', 'finished' and 'time for'. These signs will help your baby learn how to predict what is going to happen next, a crucial communication skill (see pages 10–13 and 16–17).

SOME SUGGESTED SIGNS

'MUMMY' – place central three fingers of one hand onto palm of other hand and tap twice.

'DADDY' – with index and middle finger of one hand, tap the back of the index and middle finger of other hand twice.

'GOOD' – thumb up.

'HELP' – clench fist of one hand, lay on other open flat hand, then lift slightly.

'HOME' – place finger-tips together to make roof shape.

'NAPPY' – with a flat hand, tap area of nappy on self.

'YES' – clench fist, drop wrist as if knocking on a door. Repeat.

'NO' – hold hand up, fingers together as if saying stop, and move hand briskly to side in a dismissive way.

'Mummy'   'Daddy'

'Good'   'Help'

'Home'   'Nappy'

'Yes'   'No'

Coping with change

Some complex skills that your baby needs to master

Your baby must learn that he is able to control his environment through communication and therefore doesn't need to resort to kicking and screaming. Imitation, choosing and understanding change are all skills that he will need to master if he is to understand what to do and what to say in different situations.

ENCOURAGE YOUR BABY TO IMITATE YOU

Imitating you simply means copying what you do. Babies can do this from the day they are born, but gradually they start to choose whether to copy or not. Babies need to copy facial expressions, hand and body movements as well as things like rhythms, intonation patterns and volume. Without this skill, your baby will not develop the ability to do new things. It is also important to respond positively to your baby's non-verbal communication so that he learns it has value and meaning and will want to do it again.

NOW FOCUS ON CHOOSING

An important skill that develops in the first six months is the ability to point at objects and people. When he is a bit older, this skill will help him ask for things before he can talk.

Once your baby can point at things, he will be able to start choosing. Choosing is the ability to weigh up the options and identify what you want to do. All humans become unhappy and frustrated when choice is taken away. Being able to choose will help your baby to control his life and ensure that he is happy and content. Choosing is also valuable in that it gives him the opportunity to practise giving messages – a key conversational skill that will not develop without practice.

Your baby is not born knowing how to choose. He will need to be given opportunities to learn how to choose. Start early by offering choices of food and drink, toys and clothes. Then move on to choice of games or objects or things to do or places to go.

HOW TO TACKLE CHANGE

Within a conversation, people, situations and topics can all change many times. Babies needs to learn how to deal with these changes very early in life. This may also help prevent too many tantrums when they are toddlers.

Coping with change is not as easy as it sounds, and your child needs to be able to deal with both negative and positive change. Change can cause confusion, which leads to stress and anxiety if you can't read the clues that tell you that moving from one thing to another will be OK. He will need to learn how to predict change: this develops from his ability to know when things start and finish (see pages 11–12).

sure that he learns to associate this with the idea of change. If he doesn't pick up the difficult signals for change, try using a visual clue – perhaps a card with 'oops!' written on it or a brightly coloured card in the shape of a circle or star. Every time there is a change, show the card and say 'Time to change. Now it's time for ...'

LEADING ACTIONS AND GAMES

Your baby needs to learn that he can lead activities, for example in the bath or during play. Do this by encouraging him as often as possible to ask for things by pointing or, as soon as he is able, facial expression. Always respond positively by giving him what he wants. This will encourage him to try to do it again. Your baby needs lots of practice. He must develop ways of clearly saying 'yes' and 'no' – nodding and shaking his head, for example.

A baby who finds change hard may cry a great deal, particularly in new situations. A child who can't predict change and deal effectively with it will become over-anxious during the change and may react in unexpected ways.

Make sure that change is signalled clearly. Start with positive changes. Your baby needs to be used to dealing with a happy change, such as having a treat instead of doing something else less interesting. Try taking take him to the swings when he thinks he is going to something that he doesn't like.

Early on use 'Oh dear!' to indicate a negative change, for example granny can't come or daddy is going to be late home. Make a point of linking this to doing something else that is pleasurable: 'Granny can't come, so let's go to the park.'

You will also need to help him to accept disappointment when there is no positive alternative. He might need to do this often when he is older. Make

FOCUS POINTS

★ *Help your baby copy facial expressions, gestures and so on. Have fun doing this.*

★ *Develop his pointing so he will be able to choose.*

★ *Make sure changes are signalled clearly.*

★ *Give him opportunities to take the lead in nursery rhymes and games.*

Baby starts signing too
Suddenly she can tell you what she wants

Very early in her life a baby learns how to communicate simple messages by crying, laughing, smiling and gurgling. But these are not precise methods of communicating, and your baby will show signs of frustration if you do not understand quickly enough exactly what it is that she wants. Teaching her how to make and use signs to tell you something will help to minimise her frustration and keep life calm.

SKILLS YOUR BABY MUST HAVE
There are certain things your baby must be able to do before she can begin learning to make signs.

Firstly, she must be able to understand signs (see pages 32–33).

She must also be able to look at you for more than a few seconds at a time, so that she can learn how to copy the signs you make.

She must be able to copy the actions that you make with your hands or body. Can she wave back at you? Can she copy clapping? Nursery rhymes are an excellent way to find out how well your baby can copy you.

And your baby must be able to manipulate her hands well. For example, can she isolate two fingers on one hand? Or make a pincer motion with her thumb and index finger?

HOW WILL YOUR BABY LEARN TO MAKE THE SIGNS?
As soon as you see that your baby is understanding signs, encourage her to make the signs herself – if she hasn't started already! Babies want to communicate with us and if you give them an effective way of doing so, they will. This is what to do:

❶ When your baby is screaming in her high chair and you know she understands signs such as 'drink' or 'nappy', say 'What do you want – drink or nappy?' At the same time, sign only the words 'drink' and 'nappy'. Keep things simple by giving her only two options at a time.

DOES SIGNING TEACH MY BABY OTHER SKILLS?
Because you both have to look at each other when you are signing (or you miss the sign), signing will naturally improve your baby's understanding of facial expression and body language. In order to make sense of the signs you are making, she has to focus her attention on your hands and body. At the same time, her peripheral vision will take in your face and the expressions you are making. Signing helps babies develop one of the most vital skills in successful communication, the interpretation of facial expressions and body language (see pages 28–29). It will also improve her attention and listening skills.

36

❷ Encourage her to respond by signing and saying 'Drink, yes?' ('yes' and 'no' are key signs for your baby to learn).

❸ Wait for her to copy you. If she indicates that a drink is what she wants, perhaps by pointing at the drink or getting excited, say: 'Grace, sign "drink".' If she still doesn't sign, try taking her hand and making the sign with her. Then give her the drink. Don't worry if her sign is not exactly the same as yours as long as she uses the same one each time.

If your baby is communicating well with signs, you must respond immediately. This teaches her that signing is the efficient way to communicate, and that it can be far more effective than crying. If you do not respond immediately, she will revert to screaming. The next time you go through this process, she might well sign 'drink' straightaway.

Once your baby starts to use signs, she might combine two, for example 'daddy car'. This ability is very helpful when she starts to talk. She might also use signs combined with words to communicate longer phrases, which is excellent for her language development. And she will probably develop her own signs.

Telling mum something
This baby is now a good communicator although she can't yet talk. She is telling her mother about something her mother can't see. She is signing 'Listen to the birds'.

Getting ready to talk

How to prepare for speaking

So far this book has concentrated wholly on the non-verbal skills that underpin the verbal side of communication. Here we look specifically at how to help your baby practise making sounds – by focusing on his crying, cooing and babbling – and how to encourage him when those magical first words begin to flow.

FIRST, THE CRYING

As we saw at the beginning of this book, your baby has to cry when he first starts to breathe – crying gets the vocal cords working. And with that first effort comes the start of the ability to control the breath – delicate breath control is required for speech. And it is through crying that your baby will begin learning how to change the tone of his voice – we looked at the importance of listening to your baby's cries on page 8, and on page 29 we saw how allowing him to develop varied cries expands his range of sounds.

NEXT, THE COOING AND BABBLING

As we saw on page 29, cooing and babbling represent two further stages in your baby's learning to change the sound of his voice. Cooing tends to involve vowel sounds only. Your baby will coo when he is feeling contented. He will look at you while he makes these gurgling sounds. It is important that you respond by imitating what he is doing. This will encourage him to do more cooing.

Your aim should be to help him practise making sounds – not to teach him how to say words.

Babbling develops as your baby begins to play with sounds by putting them together, for example 'ma ma'. It is quite likely that your baby will use this 'm' sound first. In the early days of his life he spends most time on his back, looking up at the world, and in this position the easiest sound to make is 'm', because all he has to do is let his lips come together and let the sound come through them. He doesn't need to move his tongue at all.

Copy me!
Mum is saying and signing, 'Look, a cat' The girl is signing and looking at the cat – soon she will say the word cat too. They are sharing information, an important skill for conversations.

However, once he can sit, his tongue will naturally fall behind the top teeth and, usually, the next sound you will hear is 'd'. Hence Mum and Dad are the names for the most important people in your baby's life!

Your baby now needs to develop fine control of his lips, tongue and soft palate, as well as his voice. All this is necessary for speech. To help him, play lots of games babbling, doing things with lips, lowering and raising the tongue in the mouth and sticking it out to point it and move it sideways. Clicks and tuts are good exercise for the tongue, too. Don't forget to use the mirror to make this more fun!

Next your aim should be to encourage him to make many different types of sounds combined with vowels. It is also important to encourage use of different speech sounds and you can do this by emphasising the vocal noises that we make during speech, for example 'daaaa', 'googoo', 'weee'. The ability to put these sounds together in the right order is a very important skill that he will need to use once he starts to talk. Once he is putting different sounds together, your baby is well on the way to saying his first word.

PUT A NAME TO EVERYTHING

To encourage your baby to start using words to communicate, you need — from a very early age — to tell him, repeatedly, the names of objects or actions. Make sure that you always use the same word for an object or action so he hears it over and over again. Eventually he will have a go at saying it himself. Gradually expand the type and range of words so he is understanding more and more words almost daily.

WHEN THE WORDS START COMING

There is a huge variation in the age at which children start to talk. As long as the non-verbal skills are developing, there is no need to worry if your baby is not talking by the time he is two or even three. You certainly do not want him to start talking too much before he is one. The shorter the time between birth and talking, the less time he will have to acquire the necessary non-verbal skills.

When he does start to say what sound like words, it is really important that you accept what he is saying even if it doesn't sound much like the target word. All you need to do is confirm what he is saying, for example, if he says 'da' for daddy and uses it regularly for daddy then all you need to do is say 'Yes, it's Daddy', so that he can hear the model of the sound he is aiming at. His listening skills are not fully developed yet and he probably thinks he is saying 'daddy'. Gradually, as he listens more carefully to how adults say his word, he will be able to make the same sound. It is important that you say these words for him over and over again in a consistent fashion to help him remember what the word sounds like.

How to talk to your baby
Keep things clear and simple

Here are some ways of talking to your baby that will
enable her to to understand you easily and will help her recognise
what different intonation patterns mean. The benefits of 'baby talk',
repetition and keeping sentences short and simple are pointed out,
as well as difficulties linked with introducing 'please' and
'thank you' too early.

HOW DO I TALK TO MY BABY?

As we saw on pages 4–5, it is important
not to talk to a baby as if she were an
adult. The language adults used in the
past when speaking to babies – 'baby
talk' – had a vital role to play. It was
instinctive, and kept ideas very simple
and at a level that a baby could pick up.

Exaggerate your tone of voice so
that your baby can learn to understand
what different intonation patterns mean.
Emphasise significant words, for example

Short and simple
This girl is pointing to some flowers. Her mother
keeps it simple by saying 'Yes, flowers' rather
than 'Yes, some pretty flowers on the piano.'

'Car goes *brmmm*', 'Door goes *bang*',
'Bye *eeeee*', '*All* gone' (with a dropping
intonation pattern). And use a sing-song
tone – '*la* di *dah* di *dah* di *dah*' – even
if the words are nonsense words, like
'coochee coochee coo'.

Reciting nursery rhymes is an excellent
way to expand your baby's understanding
of different styles of communication. By
the time she goes school, your child needs
to know that she talks to her friends in one
way, her teachers in another way, and her
family in another.

And remember: don't correct your baby
if some of her words are not perfect when
she starts talking – just model what they
should sound like (see page 39).

SHOULD I TALK IN FULL SENTENCES?

In the early days, it is best to keep to as
few words as possible: 'Mummy work',
rather than 'Mummy's gone to work now'.
Your baby will understand this more easily
than a long sentence. As it become clear
that she is able to understand more, you
can increase the number of words, for
example 'Daddy's car, it goes brmmmm'.

KEEP YOUR LANGUAGE SIMPLE

Until your child has developed a really
good understanding of grammar, it is best

to keep the words you use very simple and clear. 'It would be really nice if you could get your shoes' is much too long and complicated. 'Get your shoes' is clear and to the point. Don't worry if it sounds abrupt. In the early days getting the message is more important than learning the social niceties of communication.

DON'T ASK QUESTIONS WHEN THERE ISN'T A GENUINE CHOICE
Saying something like 'Do you want to go to bed?' when you are not really offering a choice is not a good idea because it invites the answer 'Yes' or 'No' – and you might get the answer you don't want! It is much better to tell her what is going to happen: 'It's time for bed.' This way too, she will always hear the words that go with the activity.

KEEP USING THE SAME WORDS
Your language should be consistent, as well as simple. For example, when it's bedtime, say 'Upstairs to bed', then pause and, if she doesn't go, repeat 'Upstairs to bed', pause again and, if she is still not going, say again 'Upstairs to bed'. Don't say 'Upstairs to bed' and then 'Isn't it time you went to bed?'. Babies and toddlers are not able to process a lot of words, so changing what you say is confusing.

'PLEASE' AND 'THANK YOU'
Insisting on your child saying please and thank you can block her understanding. Children do not really learn what these words mean until they are about four or five. Before that, they repeat them, learned by rote, because their parents want it and without knowing what they mean. Also, if your baby is slow to talk, she might find that saying please is a

way of getting everything she wants without needing to learn many other words. You will know when it is time to start introducing your baby to the use of please and thank you – she will be on the road to being a good communicator.

COMBINING WORDS AND SIGNS
When you sign to your baby, always say the words associated with the sign. That way, she will make connections between the sound of the word, the sign and the object, and will learn to produce it for herself more quickly.

REACT TO ACTIONS AND EVENTS
Some words seem to have gone out of common use with babies – phrases like 'Uh oh!', 'Oops a daisy', 'Yucky', 'Yum yum'. But they are very helpful for learning to understand how people are feeling. Do use them. Try this: feeling worried is an emotion your baby should learn about, so look in Margaret Miller's *Baby Faces* (see page 42) for the baby looking worried and saying 'Uh oh!'. Show your child, say 'Uh oh! *Trouble*!' and talk about why the baby might be worried. Then, when there's an accident – maybe water splashing out of the bath – say 'Uh oh! Trouble'. She will enjoy this. Try other feelings too.

FOCUS POINTS

★ *Make your message clear: be consistent in the words you use.*

★ *Model how a word should sound. Don't correct your baby.*

★ *Encourage your baby to put words and signs together.*

FURTHER READING

Author's favourites

Margaret Miller, *Baby Faces* (Simon & Schuster)

Sarah Williams and Ian Beck, *Round and Round the Garden: Play Rhymes for Young Children* (with actions) (Oxford University Press)

Annie Kubler, *My First Signs* (Child's Play)

Also recommended

Ben Argueta and Sandra Lousada, *Baby Faces* (Playskool Books)

Rosalinde Bonnet, *Nursery Rhyme Picture Book* (Usborne Picture Story Books)

Roberta Grobel Intrater, *Baby Faces* series: *Eat!/Hugs & Kisses/Peek-a-Boo!/Sleep/Smile!/Splash!* (Scholastic, Cartwheel Books)

Benedicte Guettier, *Little Players* series: *At the Circus/At the Party/In the Jungle/On the Farm/On the Move/One Scary Night/Under the Sea* (Zero to Ten)

Annie Kubler, *See-Saw! Nursery songs* (Child's Play)

Roger Priddy, *Nursery Rhymes* (Priddy Books)

NOT JUST TALKING

Not Just Talking Ltd offers assessment and intervention for children from 3 to 19 years of age who have not developed non-verbal conversational skills. Not Just Talking also provides training for parents and professionals in prevention and intervention techniques.
Please see the website for more information: www.notjusttalking.co.uk

AUTHOR'S ACKNOWLEDGEMENTS

I am particularly indebted to Sue Gordon for her belief in this book and for her tireless practical support, which has turned it into reality. I am immensely grateful to Dawn, for her commitment to the concept and her great design work; to Faye Rowe for her inspiration and encouragement; to the team at Not Just Talking, who encouraged and supported me; and to Stephen, for constant tea and sympathy.

My thanks also go to all the children and parents who helped with the photographs: Edith, Benjamin, Oliver, Isobelle, Faye, Iona, Bill, Rosie. The cover photograph is by supplied by Getty Images.

Published by Not Just Talking Ltd, 13 Lynford Way, Winchester SO22 6BW

First published in the UK in 2009
Text copyright © by Sioban Boyce

Sioban Boyce has asserted her right to be identified as author of this work in accordance with the Copyright, Designs and Patents Act, 1988.

A CIP catalogue record for this book is available from the British Library
ISBN 978-0-9558387-5-0

Produced by

OutHouse!
Winchester SO22 5DS

Designer Dawn Terrey
Editor Sue Gordon
Proofreader Stephen Boyce

Printed and bound by Sarsen Press,
22 Hyde Street, Winchester SO23 7DR
www.sarsenpress.com